THE
FCK IT
LIST

THE

F*CK IT LIST

ALL THE THINGS
YOU CAN SKIP
BEFORE YOU DIE

KEVIN PRYSLAK

VIVA
EDITIONS

Published in the United States by Cleis Press, an imprint of Start Midnight, LLC, 101 Hudson Street, Thirty-Seventh Floor, Suite 3705, Jersey City, NJ 07302.

Printed in the United States.
Cover design: Scott Idleman/Blink
Cover photograph: iStock
Text design: Frank Wiedemann

First Edition.
10 9 8 7 6 5 4 3 2

Trade paper ISBN: 978-1-63228-040-4
E-book ISBN: 978-1-63228-055-8

TABLE OF FUCK IT CONTENTS

FUCK IT:
AN INTRODUCTION

I'm sick of hearing about bucket lists. I'm sick of ambition and life goals and things people just *have* to do before they die. You know what you have to do before you die? Stop breathing. That's all. The pressure of absurd life goals will ensure that an anxiety-filled middle age ("I haven't completed enough of my bucket list yet!") will be followed by shame-filled golden years ("I'm too old to cross that off my bucket list!"). But still, bucket lists just won't go away. At some point the concept of creating these boastful to-do lists lodged itself like an arterial clog somewhere between death and taxes.

Me? I don't want to accomplish anything. Life is full enough of pressure as it is. I consider it an accomplishment if I can get to the dry cleaner and the supermarket in the same day. I say: Fuck it. I don't want to learn how to tango. I don't want to climb a volcano—on any continent. I don't want to bathe in the Ganges or run a marathon or swim with sharks. None of it. Bucket lists are a pompous and bloated rite of passage whose time has come to be gone.

That said, I have written this book as a public service to you, dear reader, to relieve you of any shame you may suffer while listening to everyone taunt you with their shining and unrealistic goals.

Go forth. Be free. Eat some ice cream and watch TV.

Kevin Pryslak

FUCK IT:
I'M NOT SETTING FOOT ON ALL SEVEN CONTINENTS

You know what everyone hears when you tell them your bucket list includes setting foot on all seven continents? Unless you're a twenty-something hipster adventurer working your way around the world on freighter ships, they hear, "I'm rich. I can do whatever I want. And *you* can't. Nyah-nyah."

To begin with, twenty-something hipsters don't think about bucket lists because they don't think about kicking the bucket. That's what makes them and their man-bun hair so annoying to the rest of us. They've yet to have their dreams die the same miserable death as Chris Christie's dignity. That aside, let's be honest: You're not really going to experience those places in any meaningful way. Sure, you'll see some cool stuff. Maybe go on one of those four-star gourmet safaris in Africa. Watch a puffin amble across a chunk of ice in the Arctic. But we all know you'll be isolated from experiencing any sort of gritty geographical reality by waiters and tour guides and hotel rooms that cost more per night than its workers earn in ten years.

The worst part, though, is that you'll be dying to tell us all about your travels—and we'll have no interest in hearing about them. Zero. In fact, after the first time—which was sort of charming and, we admit, a little inspiring—we'll secretly despise you for bringing it up again. "Did I ever tell you about the time I met the Dalai Lama?" Yeah, only ten times. Besides, waiting on line with him at McDonald's doesn't count. On the way home from listening to you, we'll make fun of how you pronounce the name of your Turkish guide, *Bünyamín*, with the proper accent. We'll unanimously decide we need to take a break from these dinners with you for a while. Eventually, we'll stop texting you altogether. You and your fucking puffins.

FUCK IT:
I'M NOT GOING TO BATHE IN THE GANGES

Hindus believe that the water of the Ganges is purifying, something that's been told to kids for thousands of years. But after cremation, the ashes of dead Hindus are thrown into the Ganges. If one is too poor to afford enough wood to incinerate the entire corpse, the ashes and whatever is left of the body are thrown into the Ganges. These ashes and body parts, combined with the feces in the river from untreated human sewage, make it one of the five most polluted rivers in the world.

As far as I'm concerned, this is a great example of an old wives' tale, or an urban legend made up by people who wanted to convince their kids to bathe in filth. It's like using Popeye to convince your kids to eat their spinach. Or telling them there's a Santa Claus to threaten them into behaving the rest of the year. I think the idea that the Ganges washes away your sins is as valid as being told masturbation will make you go blind. Hold on a second, I can't find my glasses.

I am not discounting the supernatural possibility that ten lifetimes of sins can be washed away by the waters of the Ganges for those who believe—it just pales in comparison to the gangrenous side effect. Personally, if I wanted to swim in a river of feces, I'd have booked myself on that Carnival Triumph cruise.

FUCK IT:
I'M NOT GOING TO BE IN AN ORGY

A friend of mine told me he thinks an orgy would be a great idea because it looks great in porn movies. First off, it doesn't look great in porn movies. It looks humiliating. It's demeaning enough to have to apologize for your inadequacies to one sex partner, let alone an entire committee. "Attention. Can I have your attention, please. If everyone could just drop every penis they're holding for just a moment. I just want everyone to know ... I was nervous, okay?" You know, I don't even want to sit in a movie theater eating popcorn with a bunch of strangers. Why would I want to put my mouth on them? And that's *not* butter.

FUCK IT:
I WILL NEVER INVENT ANYTHING

I'm glad I'm alive during a time when everything I'll ever need has already been invented. Anything that hasn't yet been invented is something I don't need. Once you have a computer that fits in your hand and can order everything under the sun from endless websites and apps, what more do we really need to invent? The only advances left to make are in computer technology, virtual-reality sex, and vibrator technology—and we've made tremendous advances in vibrator technology. We have remote control vibrators now. You don't even have to put your hand between your legs to masturbate anymore. God bless Japanese ingenuity.

I am very comfortable knowing I will never invent anything before I leave Pebble Earth. Although, I've been working on plans for a specially contoured car seat for people who drive with their heads up their asses. So far it involves a periscope and Vaseline.

I got the idea from a vibrator.

FUCK IT:
I'M NOT GOING TO A NUDIST COLONY

I was instilled early and often with a sense of shame about my body. In some circles, this is known as "Catholicism." I've gotten more comfortable over the years: Locker rooms are no longer an issue (with a well-placed towel), and at annual physicals I'm more concerned about my blood pressure than disrobing. And at least at a nudist colony no one is grabbing my sack and asking me to cough. But as far as I've come, I can assure you I will never be "nudist colony" comfortable with my body. Biking, cooking dinner, gardening, playing tennis, having cocktails ... all buck naked? I only wish I had the balls to pull that off.

Plus, where would I keep my cell phone?

FUCK IT:
I'M NOT GOING TO JOIN THE MILE HIGH CLUB

I can't think of anything less romantic or appealing. The "Mile High Club" was coined back when flying was luxurious. Back when people dressed up to fly like they were going to the Oscars. Back before you could fly from Rome to Pittsburgh for seven dollars. Now airplane travel is like riding on a 1947 Guatemalan bus full of people holding their chickens and assorted livestock. Babies crying. People clipping their toenails. Mothers changing diapers on their seats during lunch service—that's if you can call it lunch. They're not exactly serving raw oyster aphrodisiacs.

Nothing on a plane makes me horny. *Especially* the bathrooms. Let's just say tactfully that men in bathrooms are not real specific with their aim to begin with. Add turbulence to the situation and it's a recipe for disaster. I've given this a lot of consideration and have concluded there is no way to have sex in an airplane bathroom without at least one of the people bracing their hand on a wall. That's a long way from a rose-petal-covered bed in a romantic five-star resort. So let's file this 600 mph fantasy under "Fine in theory, hideous upon execution."

I'm pretty sure the closest I will ever get to joining the Mile High Club is if I have sex in Denver.

FUCK IT:
I'M NOT RUNNING WITH THE BULLS

In the early fourteenth century, Spaniards would jump in among the bulls to speed the process of transporting them from one place to another. It was foolhardy, but at least it served a purpose. Somewhere along the line, the Running of the Bulls was branded as a festival in honor of Saint Fermin. Do you pray to Saint Fermin? Oh wait, you've never *heard* of Saint Fermin? Well, let me enlighten you. He was beheaded. That's all you need to know. It's reported that at his burial the sick were healed and trees mysteriously bowed in his direction, but let's stay on task here. Running with the bulls was made world famous in the 1920s when Ernest Hemingway chronicled it in *The Sun Also Rises*. Running with the bulls is mere foreplay to the full-tilt orgy known as bullfighting which, as you know, is a PETA nightmare that ends with the bloody killing of the bull. So how far are you willing to take this dance with death? Will you stop at "the running" so that you can duck into a safety barricade whenever danger comes too close and try to avoid losing a dangling foot in the process? Or will you get down in the thick of it and make your *estocada* thrust into the heart of a beast whose only crime is *really* liking the color red?

FUCK IT:
I'M NOT GOING TO DRINK TIGER'S MILK IN AN ASHRAM

It has been said that tiger's milk is so potent that only a pure golden vessel can contain it. Any lesser container would be eaten through, leaving a steaming puddle of tiger's milk on the floor. This nugget of dubious wisdom is most commonly conveyed by a guru to budding yogis as a message about strengthening the vessel (the body of the yogi) so that it can hold the energy generated by meditation, yoga, study, and contemplation. Indian ashrams are a hotbed for neat little parables that must be taken on faith. I have faith that my vessel will never be full of milk from the teat of a man-eating beast. Unless you stir in some Hershey's syrup.

FUCK IT:
I'M NOT SWIMMING WITH SHARKS

Six words: "We're gonna need a bigger boat." Listing swimming with sharks on your bucket list is extremely close to having "being eaten alive by sharks" included on your bucket list. Maybe that's the allure. You tempt death. You get to look millions of years of evolution of nature's greatest killing machine directly in its cold black eyes and taunt it with "See these? Opposable thumbs. Helps us build shark cages." But you're not in a shark cage, are you? Because you're a moron. You are *swimming with* the sharks. You are their main course. You know what you should have on your bucket list? "Make it to the end of my life without being featured on a menu." At the very least, post this one as the last item on your bucket list, because it's highly unlikely you will scratch off any more goals after you are spewed from a shark's alimentary canal.

FUCK IT:
I'M NOT GOING TO CLIMB MOUNT EVEREST

When he was asked by a reporter why he wanted to climb Mount Everest, mountaineer George Mallory replied, "Because it's there." This might be a good time to remind yourself there are also a lot of "elsewheres." You could also sail on a nice quiet lake with a picnic basket and a bottle of wine because it's there. This bright expeditionary idea begs the question, "Where would my money, or, more likely, my rich daddy's inheritance, be better spent?" If I had the money—which seems to be anywhere from $50,000–$100,000 depending on the guide company and package—I'd give it straight to the Sherpas to build another Buddhist monastery so they can spend more time enlightening and less time schlepping some rich thrill-seeker's shit up a 29,029 foot cliff.

People who want to climb Everest say it's a personal challenge. You know what else is a personal challenge? Not freezing your ass off for two weeks with no oxygen just so you can go to swank dinner parties for the rest of your life playing the role of the awesome guy who climbed Mount Everest. "Yep. That's me. *Mount Everest.* Can someone cut my steak for me? I lost my fingers from frostbite."

FUCK IT:
I'M NOT VOLUNTEERING FOR SPACEX

Google "SpaceX." There are 21,300,000 results. The first result is the headline "First SpaceX missions to Mars: 'Dangerous and probably people will die.'"

Dying is not on my bucket list. By definition. And there are physical requirements to make the Mars trip. I'd have to be healthy. I'd have to do sit-ups. I'd have wires hooked up to me. I'd have to shit in a bag. Weightlessly. And this, again, is all for bragging rights. And if, by remote chance, I don't die, who's going to be impressed? The people I climbed Everest with?

FUCK IT:
I'M NOT GOING TO LEARN A NEW LANGUAGE

How much Spanish or French do you remember from high school? Is the president about to appoint you ambassador to another country? No? Are you going to teach English as a second language in Uganda? No?

There are phone apps for this. The only reason to learn a country's native language is to show respect to them. But really, why would you want to learn French, for example? The French already assume Americans are rude and stupid so that one's a pyrrhic victory. You don't need to know how to conjugate irregular verbs in another language to find out where the bathroom is. It's often said that you'll know you've mastered a foreign language when you can dream in that language. I say sex with a supermodel is still sex with a supermodel even in Swahili.

FUCK IT:
I'M NOT GOING TO TAKE A PICTURE
EVERY DAY FOR A YEAR

There are the trips to the Pacific Ocean, breathtaking sunsets, and your child's first smile that wasn't caused by gas. But those events are few and far between. If your posts on Facebook are any indication, you lead a pretty mundane life. And I'm being gracious by not saying your life is downright boring. We don't adore your cat anywhere near as much as you do. In fact, we're a little concerned about the extent to which you're fond of your cat—and I guarantee your cat is not as fond of you as you are of him. We also think you're delusional if you expect that your Farmville high score screen grab will grab us. And if I see one more picture of the meal you had for dinner last night, I'm going to reply with a photo of what my last meal looked like coming out the other end.

FUCK IT:
I'M NOT GOING TO GET MY EAR/
TONGUE/NIPPLE/NOSE PIERCED

Around ninth grade (1984), the first wave of ear piercings washed up on the shores of my adolescence, carrying with it the faint briny tang of sexual awakening. Ear piercing was cutting edge then. There doesn't seem to be much difference between ear/tongue/nipple/nose or any other type of piercing at this point, though. The zesty thrill of originality is gone. The aura of rebellion has vanished. With the advent of people coming to their senses and allowing others to do whatever and whomever they want, the secret code about which ear "meant you were gay" is no longer necessary. Thankfully, my parents were able to exert their will on me just long enough to prevent me from making the holiest of mistakes. I've seen parents who pierce their daughters' ears when they're two months old. There's something very weird about seeing a two-year-old girl with Dora the Explorer earrings. And, while I'm at it, if you have a chain that goes from your nose piercing to your ear piercing, you should at least hang a sign from it and sell advertising space, because people *are* going to stare.

FUCK IT:
I'M NOT GOING TO LEARN HOW TO PAINT

This one falls under the category of "If you didn't learn it when you were young, you're not going to get good at it now." Unless of course you have so much time on your hands after you retire that you need to come up with something to avoid listening to your spouse of fifty years talking nonstop about the church bake sale and who just got a disease and who just died. No one should dabble in the arts. To paint, draw, photograph, write poems, stories, novels, only to impose upon your friends to ask them what they think and to "please, be honest," is cruel and, unfortunately, all-too-usual punishment. I will not "try my hand" at painting because no one should "try their hand" at anything artistic.

And let's face it, you are definitely never going to make money from painting. You know who started painting late in life? John Wayne Gacy and Charles Manson. Gacy painted clowns. Like clowns don't scare kids enough already. Manson paints and makes spider sculptures out of string and human hair. And people *buy* them. So unless you add "killing people" to your bucket list, your "artwork" won't be worth a Manson parole hearing.

FUCK IT:
I'M NOT GOING TO BECOME A MILLIONAIRE

The American Dream, for all intents and purposes, is dead. Or, generously, it's in a coma. Immigrants show up lucky to mow a lawn, drive a cab, or wash some dishes. What chance do you have?

This is a great lesson in acceptance. I've run through my options. The older you get, the less opportunities you have. Most people who are rich have gotten there quicker than they could say, "My father went to Yale with your father." A few lucky people get rich by inventing something. But there are a lot of hopeful people out there holding on to the dream that their ship will come in. And God bless optimism. But for me, the American Dream has been relegated to the fantasy of buying a winning lottery ticket—and that dream dies every night at 9:00 p.m. I hate to be cynical, but embracing my cynicism would be on my bucket list if I had one.

FUCK IT:
I'M NOT GOING TO LEARN HOW TO FLY A PLANE

I'm what you might call a "nervous flier." Not the ostentatious kind who twiddles his rosary beads and rocks back and forth, but I'm not happy to be in a metal tube hurtling through the sky faster than a disgruntled CEO can ruin a Fortune 500 company. I used to get bad panic attacks at the very thought of sitting in my tiny little seat and being strapped into a fuselage for even forty-five minutes. There was something about that ultimate containment with nowhere to escape to that churned my guts like razorblade marbles. With the help of time—and most notably, Xanax—I've overcome that sphincter-tightening panic, but still, who knows when it might come back? Would you like to be flying with me if it did? Me on Xanax? As your pilot?

FUCK IT:
I'M NOT GOING TO LEARN TO PLAY GOLF

Oh, where do I begin? First off, no matter what you say, golf is not a sport. Golf is a sport like darts is a sport. If golf is a sport, then raking leaves is a sport. Oh, you can pretend you're getting exercise while a caddy is carrying your bag as you ride along from green to green on a golf cart with a Rolls Royce grill. But your belly hanging over your nine iron tells a different story.

Not to mention, that belly is hanging out of a pink shirt. A big-bellied pink shirt stuffed into pants with prints of little whales and sailboats on them. This is a good time to mention that the word "golf" originated as an acronym for "Gentlemen Only, Ladies Forbidden." After all, who can concentrate on golf with a gallery of women giggling at the absurdity of men dressed like clowns desperately trying to hit a ball into a hole with a stick?

Most women could not care less about golf. You could be the best golfer in the world and your wife's only concern would be which one of your clubs to use to bash the windshield on your Cadillac Escalade.

To me, perhaps the only thing goofier than playing golf is watching golf on television. There is actually a Golf Channel. Twenty-four hours of golf. What could be more boring than watching golf on TV? Watching *reruns* of golf on TV. That's what.

Also, no one is ever "good at golf"—you can always get better. In fact, it's always practice, it's always rehearsal. A bunch of men cursing out their luck. Probably the only thing golf is good for is making business deals. You invite a client out to golf and you let him win. Because, of course, a little dishonesty is the foundation for all good business deals.

Dating back hundreds of years, golf has been dubbed "the game of kings." You know what else was a popular game of kings? Starving out the people living on their lands. Probably to make room for a golf course.

FUCK IT:
I'M NOT LEARNING HOW TO TANGO

As far as I can tell, taking dance lessons with your partner (actually, taking any lessons at all with your partner) is code for "our marriage sucks." I must say, though, Robert Duvall makes this look very appealing. Duvall took his *Godfather* money and used it to travel all over the world to tango with his South American wife, and they are good! Almost good enough to make this look appealing. Almost. But if you are in a marriage and you ask your partner if she wants to learn how to tango, you are throwing down the spicy gauntlet. *We need to do this thing together or I will do it with a different partner.* You're probably better off line dancing your way to couples counseling first.

FUCK IT:
I'M NOT RECONNECTING WITH A
HIGH SCHOOL SWEETHEART

So, if I'm following correctly, here's the idea. You follow said sweetheart on social media, and, after your wife and kids are asleep, you peruse her full online life of kids, sports, regular trips with a hint—just a taste—of adventure. Your life falls and rises, collapses and rides out torturous doldrums. But, through it all, there is this sweetheart out there who maybe once said something nice . . . or lived next door . . . or maybe even let you touch her boobies. Here's something very important to understand: This is all in your imagination. There's a difference between nostalgia and delusion. If you get to the point where you find yourself wondering what your kids might have looked like, you're officially creepy. There's a fine line between curiosity and stalking.

FUCK IT:
I'M NOT TAKING A HELICOPTER TOUR OF A VOLCANO

No one ever mentions updrafts and downdrafts on the brochure. Not to mention you have one blade holding you up—and it's spinning. I've had my car stall on I-80. I limped it over to the side of the road. What I didn't do was plummet to the ground and burst through the roof of a shack in Louisiana at terminal velocity like a hundred-pound frozen crap-meteorite from a 747.

Am I the only one who imagines an explosive geyser of lava shooting out of the mouth of the volcano and melting the helicopter? I try my best to picture it like that opening sequence in *Magnum P.I.* where they're swooping down over the ocean in Hawaii and everything is sexy and sunny and filled with chest hair and sunglasses. But as soon as we add "volcano" to "helicopter" my mind goes straight to being melted alive in a 2,120-degree tragedy, with my pair of cheap aviator sunglasses fused to my face for eternity and a day.

FUCK IT:
I'M NOT MENTORING ANYONE

In theory, I love the idea of "paying it forward." Spiritual para-
doxes like "you have to give it away to keep it" or "the love you
take is equal to the love you make" occasionally float through my
mind like the smile of an old lover. It would be nice having someone following me around, hanging on to my every word like I've
got directions to a buried treasure. As my protégé you would lean
in close and listen while calculating what to say to make the best
impression. And I imagine my truths would be cosmic, timeless,
like those of a Zen master.

Yes, I would love to be feel connected to the time continuum,
knowing a part of me was living on through someone who values
all that I am. But I don't know anything.

FUCK IT:
I'M NOT FIREWALKING

Firewalking—which dates back to 1200 BCE—has been taken up by corporations as a "team building" exercise. The corporate training arm of this ancient ritual was dealt a blow in 2002 when twenty managers from Kentucky Fried Chicken were treated for firewalk-related burns in Australia. Still, thanks to Tony Robbins, the industry continues to thrive. Even after thirty people at one of his seminars reported burns on their feet, who knows how much longer it will last? I'm content with having traversed scorching-hot pavement with an oversized umbrella and two folding chairs while holding the ice-cream-sticky hands of screaming children, dodging cars and remaining bent on eliminating a suburban cliché. I won't walk barefoot on burning coals, lie down on a bed of nails, or walk on broken glass. These are not examples of mind over matter. Your skin doesn't care what your mind thinks. And neither does Tony Robbins.

FUCK IT:
I'M NOT LEARNING HOW TO THROW A POT

Right after the movie *Ghost* came out, people everywhere started taking pottery classes because Patrick Swayze and Demi Moore made it look so sensuous. There's something you need to know: Back then, Patrick Swayze and Demi Moore could have made dumpster diving look sexy.

You've seen it: the adult versions no better than third-grade art project results, the impression of every little finger still visible no matter how much you tried smoothing the sides with that Popsicle stick thing. And the glaze: always vaguely poop-colored and slathered six applications too deep. Heaven forbid you attempt a coffee cup—those ones with a barely stuck-on cauliflower-ear of a handle that comes loose as soon as it's grasped. And thank God the things are useless, because we can only speculate what chemical reactions must occur when a hot liquid hits that thick chemical glaze. No, I don't want to learn how to throw a pot of any kind. The only thing I've ever made from clay is a handprint in kindergarten. And it was off-center.

FUCK IT:
I'M NOT GOING TO SAVE UP FOR A MAUSOLEUM

I've never been able to zero in on my preferred method of post-mortem disposal. The thought of having my ashes sprinkled over the Rhine conjures a beautifully Teutonic scene pervaded by *The Flying Dutchman* overture, but the idea of being burned up makes my balls tingle in the bad way.

Mausoleum? Even the language—Latin—is dead. How about a sarcophagus? How about a pyramid? Or being buried with your cat like Ramses II? Who cares, really? Who's going to see your mausoleum? When's the last time you went sightseeing in a cemetery? Maybe, if you're lucky, once a year your kids might come around and curse you out for spending $100,000 to climb Mt. Everest, leaving them nothing but a mausoleum to visit.

FUCK IT:
I'M NOT GOING TO PUNXSUTAWNEY
FOR GROUNDHOG DAY

The fact that this is even an event is a testament to small-town survival. Pennsylvania's earliest settlers were German. The Romans, who had conquered the Teutons (who were the precursors to Germans), held a belief that if a hedgehog saw its shadow on Candelmas—February 2, "The Purification of the Virgin"—it would mark the start of the "Second Winter," or, in our parlance, "six more weeks of winter." Thus German settlers, via their Teutonic ancestors, having settled in Pennsylvania, saw groundhogs as close kin to hedgehogs, and carried this ancient Roman practice of weather prediction into modern day. In 1886, *The Punxsutawney Spirit*, the paper of record for the region, noted in its February 2 issue, "Today is Groundhog Day, and up to the time of going to press the beast has not seen his shadow." Punxsutawney became ground zero for Groundhog Day and would feature an official groundhog, Punxsutawney Phil; an official viewing site, ingloriously named Gobbler's Knob (not to be confused with the porn video, *Knob Gobblers*); and tens of thousands of visitors who converge on Punxsutawney on February 2, providing local newscasters from TV Station KNOB their annual big moment in the sun. Or the shade. Depending.

FUCK IT:
I'M NOT GOING TO PROVE A CONSPIRACY THEORY

Dear Facebook Conspiracy Theorist,

If you're convinced there's a "real story" behind some major event, it's not going to be a "real story" revealed by you or anyone you interact with on social media. Because you're not that smart.

Look around you. Look at your life. Look at your mobile home. Look at the broken washing machine in your front yard, overgrown with weeds. Look at your below-average offspring. If there's any big plot to be uncovered, you are obviously not the one with the cunning and intellect to figure it out. So stop already.

FUCK IT:
I'M NOT GOING TO BE ON A GAME SHOW

When I was growing up I used to look forward to watching *Let's Make a Deal* with Monty Hall. So much fun seeing the audience dressed like vegetables and hillbillies awaiting their chance to trade everything for Carol Merrill's box.

Nowadays, every morning in Los Angeles you can drive by CBS Studios and see the lines filled with midwestern tourists waiting for a chance to be a contestant on *The Price is Right*. They're out there, each hoping against hope to be the lucky one chosen to assess a washer/dryer at a dollar less than the contestant before them. The best part is watching the contestant who just got screwed by that bid give the other guy the stink-eye.

My brightest memories of game shows involve Bob Barker yelling, "Come on down!" My darkest memories are of people in too-tight shirts and mullets bounding down the aisle like stuffed sausages descending an escalator.

FUCK IT:
I'M NOT GETTING BACK IN SHAPE

If I got back in shape every time I thought I should get back in shape I'd be built like Schwarzenegger. I keep telling myself I will. It's a sickness, really. A form of psychosis.

It's true—I was in shape at one time. I didn't exactly have a six-pack, but there was a straighter, less bulbous line between my lower abdomen and chest. What was once a distinct butt, thighs, back, and waist are now a gelatinous mess, but my girlfriend's fantasy is bathing in a Jell-O moat surrounding an adequately sized castle—so we're good.

FUCK IT:
I'M NOT GOING TO MASTER THE RUBIK'S CUBE

The Rubik's cube hit the world in 1980. Since then, every conceivable element of difficulty has been tried. I've seen the videos. 4 x 4 x 4, 5 x 5 x 5, 6 x 6 x 6, 7 x 7 x 7. Solving while skydiving. Kids solving it blindfolded. Guinness lists records for robots solving the cube. It's insane. While I'm sure it's fun for the people who need something to do during the fifty weeks of the year between Comic-Cons, it's not for me. When I was young enough to have free time for impossible puzzles, I was trying to solve puzzles called "girls." (I own the record for the longest duration not solving that puzzle.) Besides, let's face it: As far as fads go, most people would be lucky to master the Pet Rock.

FUCK IT:
I'M NOT GOING TO THE NORTH POLE

I was chatting with some perfectly nice people at a holiday party, and asked them what was on their bucket lists, not divulging the book I was researching nor my intention to put their dreams through a rusty blender. I waited until I deemed them soused enough to get friendly with a tattooed stranger, and one apple-cheeked, be-sweatered, overly spirited woman gave me an author's diamond-studded Christmas gift: "Well I'd like to go to the North Pole!" She said it just like that, exclamation point and all. The diamonds were the earnest description of a land where the Christmas spirit lives year-round: elves, reindeer, and the whole nine yards. I tried to be respectful, I did, she was just so adorable, but when she started to divine baking Christmas cookies with Mrs. Claus, I blurted out with what I thought, *wrongly*, as it turns out, was a very clever Christmastime response: "What are you, a fruitcake?" Her whole head turned Rudolph-nose red, and others who had unwittingly participated in my little literary social experiment looked at me like

I had just pissed in their eggnog, but I had a holiday addition to *The Fuck It List* and a marketing hook for the publisher to advertise it as a stocking stuffer. Guess who's getting coal in his stocking? Me.

FUCK IT:
I'M NOT GOING TO KISS THE BLARNEY STONE

The Blarney Stone, located at Blarney Castle, is also known as "The Stone of Eloquence." Not that the Irish really need it. Who's more eloquent than an Irishman with a few stouts in his belly? Irish lore holds that kissing the Blarney Stone will endow one with the gift of eloquence and the ability to "deceive without offending." We have another term for this in America. It's called "politics." And every single politician can kiss my Blarney ass.

FUCK IT:
I'M NOT GETTING A BLACK BELT IN TAE KWON DO

Just once—but of course, only when justified by the pursuit of truth, justice, and the American way—I'd like to beat the hell out of someone. But I'm just too squeamish for that. I've always found myself a chicken-shit way to deescalate tense situations by asking morally industrious questions like, "What's on *your* bucket list?" So what's the point of spending all those hours mastering tae kwon do? Oh I know, I know: It's not *about* fighting. It's about learning discipline and strengthening body and mind and all that. But really, if I'm going to spend time learning how to punch and kick, I'm damn well going to use it to deliver a solid ass-whooping to someone who deserves it. But, like I said, I'm a chicken shit. Er, uh, I mean, "pacifist."

FUCK IT:
I'M NOT GOING TO BUILD MY OWN HOUSE

We all have different skill sets. Some people are musically inclined, some are endowed with personal charisma, some are math and science wizzes, and some have the ability to build things with their hands. I am not a builder. In fact, I come from a long line of people who repaired things using all the wrong materials. My grandfather, a dentist, used to fix everything with a pink dental adhesive he referred to as "crabbles." Nearly every nonperishable item in his home had at least a small dab of crabbles on it somewhere keeping it together. My people are the ones who use duct tape and the wrong kinds of screws. We fix things until they're "good enough" as opposed to "fixed." So you can only imagine what my self-built house would look like—the wrong angles, slanting floorboards, six-inch gaps beneath the walls. So, how about you let me build *your* house?

FUCK IT:
I'M NOT GOING TO TRY A CIVIL WAR REENACTMENT

Motivated by temporary escape from being a functioning adult, I actually looked into this and almost decided to begin my Union soldier training—until I discovered that the war that raged beneath wasn't really about the Unions and Confederates, but the most authentic reenactors and what the devout call "Mainstream." They're good enough at reenacting, sure, but the "Hardcores"— also know as "Stitch Counters"—maintain that if you look closely enough you'll find a Fruit of the Loom tag sticking out the back of someone's Confederate trousers, or you'll spot an anachronistic hairstyle. I could deal if the battlefield was the Internet and the haters a few trolls, but I got wind of accounts where calling someone out for having a "Bieber" resulted in a run-through with a bayonet. Plus, there's the category of pretenders that I would no doubt fall into: "Farbs." Farbs are the lowest rung of Civil War reenactors. They may wear sneakers and jeans or synthetic fabrics tossed together with a piece or two of authentic gear, and then go sneak a Marlboro after they're killed. Not to mention the ultimate anachronism: these guys pulling out their cell phones for realistic 1865 Matthew Brady sepia-toned selfies. Or furiously Googling the word "anachronism" for that matter. These are the people who aren't hip enough to go to Comic-Con. This activity is definitely not a great way to meet chicks; I'd advise you don't boast this on your eHarmony profile. What I'd really like to see is these guys reenacting "The Battle of Getting My Mom to Let Her Thirty-Five-Year-Old Son Live in Her Basement." I'd pay good Confederate money to see that.

FUCK IT:
I'M NOT GETTING A COFFEE ENEMA

There are a whole lot of people who swear this is a great idea for your health. I was at a dinner party one night and the topic came up. And when I say "came up," I mean there was a woman there who was into holistic stuff. She was wearing crystals and smelled strongly of patchouli oil. Apparently she was compelled to believe that somewhere in between the main course and dessert would be a perfect time to talk about irrigating her digestive system. She began excitedly telling everyone about how wonderful coffee enemas are. "It's a powerful detoxifier! It's great for your colon and your kidneys and your liver!"

My first instinct was to suggest she switch her enemas to decaf, but I stifled the impulse.

Did I mention she was sitting next to me? When none of the ten people at the table engaged her discussion, I became the targeted personal beneficiary of her fount of wisdom. (Yes, I chose the word 'fount' on purpose. Not to mention this topic gives new meaning to the term "bucket list.") When she began informing me of the specifics of administering said alimentary treat, I cut her short by telling her, "I'll try a coffee enema when they offer it at Starbucks."

FUCK IT:
I'M NOT DOING A POLAR BEAR SWIM

Perhaps you've never heard of the Polar Bear Swim. Every New Year's Day beginning in 1920, The Polar Bear Swim Club in British Columbia, Canada, holds its annual swim. Now it's done all over the world. Some of these events take place when the temperature is twenty-five degrees below zero. Polar Bear Swims across the world boast hundreds, sometimes thousands of participants, with as many as ten thousand spectators—who are also known as "the sane ones." Many of these masochists fill their gullets with booze before they do it, although they prefer to call it antifreeze. Some refer to it as the "Watch Your Testicles Disappear Swim." But the good Lord has ways of balancing things out, because it also makes for some rock-hard nipples. That probably explains the ten thousand spectators. In Russia, these plunges are pursued as a process of strengthening oneself—they call it "hardening." Irony, anyone?

FUCK IT:
I'M NOT SKYDIVING

High-place phenomenon is not a fear of heights. It's the feeling that people—myself included—get when they're in high places and are afraid they have a desire to jump. I repeat: It is the fear of the desire to jump. Weird, right? Apparently, it is not an urge for self-destruction, but an instinct for self-preservation. It is related to "high anxiety sensitivity." HPP can best be understood by example: A person—let's call them "you"—reaches the highest point on a Ferris wheel. You look over the edge and your brain goes through three instantaneous processes balanced between healthy survival instincts and high anxiety sensitivity. You instinctually shrink back in fear because, in truth, falling from such a height would kill you. You realize that you are safely buckled into a steel seat and that you are not in imminent danger. Your anxious brain wonders if your fear was, in fact, an urge to throw yourself past the twinkling carnival lights into a splat beside the cotton candy stand. That, my friend, is human nature. But wanting to throw yourself from an airplane before you die is not human nature—it's hubris. Who are you to defy two hundred thousand years of time-tested survival instincts?

But here's my biggest fear about skydiving: disgruntled employees. Taking people skydiving is a job. People snap at their jobs all the time. Like the guy who gets caught on a hidden security video peeing in the office coffee pot. What if the guy who packs my chute decides that's a good day for workplace violence? I'm not sacrificing my life just to provide his neighbors the opportunity to tell a news crew, "He was a quiet man."

FUCK IT:
I'M NOT GOING TO POP A WHEELIE ON A MOTORCYCLE

Four wheels on a vehicle are nice and sturdy. I like that a lot. Two wheels are acceptable but not ideal. I like that less. One wheel? I don't think so.

Motorcycles have their appeal. Wind blowing through your hair. A chick on the back with her arms wrapped around you. You're a bit of an outlaw, something like Marlon Brando in *The Wild Ones*. So I get it. But there have been a few times I've been driving my car down the freeway, safely and quite happily surrounded by steel armor, and suddenly a motorcycle will pass me at 80 mph. That sight is bad enough to get a flash of concern for the rider. But then, and you may have seen this, the moron, wearing shorts and a T-shirt, mind you, lifts the front wheel off the ground. *At 80 miles an hour!* Life can be scary enough without that big of a "fuck you" to death. If you've gotten to the point where that's the edge you need to find to be excited with life, you may not be long for this Earth. If I had a bucket list, "not dying while trying to impress people I don't know" would be at the top of that list.

FUCK IT:
I'M NOT GOING TO OPEN A NEIGHBORHOOD TAVERN

Owning a neighborhood tavern is like having a shitty job—the worst part of having a shitty job is not *doing* the shitty job, it's having to hang out with other people who couldn't get a better job than this. You have no control over who decides your bar is going to be their regular hangout. Do you want to spend your days and nights listening to alcoholics talk about the time something good almost happened to them? Or their dreams of riches? Or complaining about their marriages? Or dissecting their suck-ass football team's chances to make it to the Super Bowl? Or giving you their political conspiracy theories? Fucking *politics*? It's enough to drive a man to drink. So there you are, eight o'clock in the morning, handing a pickled egg and a depth charge to a quivering Wal-Mart Charles Bukowski, making change for the pool table, and fielding phone calls from a twelve-year-old girl wondering where her daddy is, wishing all the while you had a neighborhood tavern you could head to so you could plop yourself down on a barstool and bitch at the barkeep about how much owning a neighborhood tavern sucks.

FUCK IT:
I'M NOT GOING TO READ ALL OF SHAKESPEARE'S PLAYS

All props to Shakespeare, whoever he is. I've got my copy of *The Riverside Shakespeare* from college and the sonofabitch is 1,927 pages long. That's 1,927 pages of Elizabethan English that you need a special dictionary to even understand at this point. Though without consulting it, I'm sure Willie would understand, *Sucketh my codpiece, I've got Netflix motherfucker* . . . I mean, *Oedipus*.

FUCK IT:
I'M NOT RESOLVING OLD GRIEVANCES

One way I have encouraged myself to grow up is to separate per-
ceived grievances from a true instance of being shit on. This took
some doing. I've always had a strong reaction to injustice and some
of my best FU stances have been based on indignation or resent-
ment stemming from a feeling of having been wronged. However,
feeling aggrieved can be habit-forming. Righteous indignation is
the narcissist's speedball: the perfect combination of angry adrenaline and the soothing self-satisfaction that comes with having your
worldview affirmed (yes, Virginia, the world is out to get you). So
shedding the narcissism of youth can be difficult, but also reward-
ing. You can learn to find pleasure in less hate-based ways that
don't ultimately scald your insides into a Mordor-like wasteland.
The flip side is that now you can really narrow in on the fuckers
with whom who you've got a legitimate beef. Revenge is a dish best
served like a laser-guided missile.

FUCK IT:
I'M NOT GOING TO THE KENTUCKY DERBY

Horse racing is a sport for rich people. The "upper crust." Old millionaires with their trophy horses and trophy wives. I am not a rich person. I have never dated a woman who has to decide which one of her thirty flowery bonnets she'll wear to "the big event of the social season."

The Kentucky Derby has been running since 1875. It's a tradition. *The Run for the Roses*. Basically, it's a big deal because people have made it a big deal. The weeks prior to the race are full of anticipation, partying, and speculation. All this hoopla and buildup for an event that's going to be over in a mere two minutes? I'll bet the trophy wives can relate to that.

FUCK IT:
I'M NOT GOING TO STUDY WITH A GURU

I awoke one morning with a vision of myself standing on a beach in California. My back was to the ocean and my chest was facing due east. There were beams of light emanating from my heart and blazing across the country lighting up thousands of dark souls like candles as my white light flew unimpeded and soaked into the deepest crevices of desire, need, and want. It turned those cravings inside out until each soul became a candle of its own, lighting up those around them until no darkness remained. We all saw ourselves as the gurus that we are and a bunch of motherfuckers in saffron robes were out of their jobs.

FUCK IT:
I'M NOT GOING TO START A BAND

The last book I wrote had me spending a couple years interviewing touring musicians in various and sundry backstage areas and tour buses. I'm not going to tell you about the grind of touring, the long hours of anonymity followed by the surreal adrenaline blast of performance, the crappy fried food and the bass player's sour farts. No, that's all well-documented and perhaps part of the allure. The reason I'm not going to start a band is because today's musicians, by and large, are a really boring lot. Honestly, sitting in an airport watching travelers fiddle fixedly on their phones is pretty much a carbon copy of modern backstage areas. This ain't 1970s Led Zeppelin humping their Starship airplane across America in a cloud of teenage ass and blow, kiddos. The groupies have joined the PTA and there are better drugs to be had in the neighbor's medicine cabinet. There is no better example of age killing a dream than the idea of being a rock star. All you have to do is go to a Bobby Vinton concert and watch the seventy-five-year-old women throwing their bras and panties at the stage. Caveat emptor.

FUCK IT:
I'M NOT GOING TO SWIM WITH DOLPHINS

This is the PG version of swimming with sharks. Fun for the whole family! When I think of dolphins, I picture them swimming free, jumping out of the water, flying through the air. And frolicking. Dolphins love to frolic. Dolphins in a pool don't frolic. They languish. While having their dorsal fins grabbed a hundred times a day by tourists. Just ask yourself, if dolphins had bucket lists, do you think swimming with you would be on it?

And while I'm at it, I can't decide which Bahamas tourist attraction I feel sorrier for, the dolphins, or the horse-drawn carriages. Skanky horses pulling wagons that look like they've been through a dozen hurricanes. Notice they call them "horse-drawn carriages." In New York City they're called "handsome carriages." In the Bahamas they just drop any pretense. Calling them "handsome" would be like naming a war "civil."

FUCK IT:
I'M NOT GOING TO TIMES SQUARE ON NEW YEAR'S EVE

When I was younger, the very idea of New York City terrified me. It was the 1970s and I had seen *Taxi Driver*. It was harrowing. It didn't help that in my late teens, during my first trip to the big city, I gave money to a random guy on the street to buy me beer and he bolted into the night. (Yeah, that one's on me.) It's for those reasons that I'll never go to Times Square for New Year's Eve. The idea calls back all those old fearful memories—all the clutter, barely veiled urine smell, lurking pickpockets—but wrapped in glittery party hats and the collective overenthusiasm that makes the big shining ball dropping from the sky look like one of King Kong's testicles dangling from the Empire State Building, lit up like a syphilitic Christmas tree.

FUCK IT:
I'M NOT GOING TO MARRY RICH

On the contrary, I should find a dirt-poor girl to marry. We could clip coupons together and squirrel away our pennies for that new recliner we've dreamed about. The one that would sit in front of the TV we'd have one day and the cable channels we'd order eventually. We would dream big and work hard and I'd be a constant reminder to my beloved Cinderella that things could always get worse.

FUCK IT:
I'M NOT GOING TO UFO WATCH

Though I would volunteer to get beamed into one. I'd look the little green weirdos right in their oversized eyes, energetically shake their three-fingered hands, and even undergo all their tests—I bet the shit they give you to numb the anal probe is out of this world. If you're an alien reading this, "weirdo" is just another way of saying "esteemed guests." And "Kevin Pryslak" is the leader to whom you should ask other earthlings to take you.

Although, I would love to see Howard Stern get abducted by aliens who then, smiling wryly, would ask him, "Do you do anal?"

FUCK IT:
I'M NOT GOING TO TRY EAR CANDLING

"Ear candling" (also known as "ear coning" or, for you fancy types, "thermal auricular therapy") was some marketing genius's idea to sell candles as part of an ancient Hopi spiritual treatment and, boom, suddenly sticking lit candles in one's ear was akin to the equally dubious practices of sweating it out in a tent, petting fawns, and mud-bathing under the guidance of a shaman in the Peruvian jungle. The Hopis never stuck lit candles in *their* ears. To my knowledge, they did not engage in trepanning (also known as "trephination," "trephining," or, if you kick it old school, making a "burr hole") either. Trepanning is the process of drilling a hole into one's head (or having a trusted professional/idiot friend do so) to release evil spirits, cure seizures, heal mental illness and generally support the good health that has afforded you the uncomfortably large amount of time you have on your hands, which would be better spent in a meditation class where you might meet some hippie chick to play with your love candle.

FUCK IT:
I'M NOT GOING TO WRITE THE GREAT AMERICAN NOVEL

There was a dream that was writing the Great American Novel, but now that dream is gone along with all the writers who drank themselves to death in the 1950s trying to get there. The average American can't differentiate between "push" and "pull" on a door. Very few people read novels since the advent of the Internet. Ninety percent of people can't get all the way through a meme.

FUCK IT:
I'M NOT GOING TO BE AN EXTRA ON A TV SHOW

I was walking through Times Square last Thanksgiving and came across a clump of tourists jumping up and down, waving their arms and smiling like they'd just had their butts tickled by the holy feather of the Lord. I took a look around and realized they were—at that very moment—on live TV, unwitting dupes on some show that kept cutting to a Times Square camera in-between whatever else they were doing. And these folks were thrilled to death to have their smiling faces on live TV. "What show you on?" I asked a particularly enthusiastic lady, whose voluptuous chest curbed some of my condescension for what this bouncing collective was doing. "I don't know!" she declared wildly, undeterred, like she was in the throes of some Dionysian fantasy. But she was so happily convinced of something that my mood turned existentialist and I started to question not just the enterprise, but who was *really* the dope—me or her?

FUCK IT:
I'M NOT GOING TO VISIT CELEBRITY GRAVE SITES

Whatever made these people famous in the first place is best appreciated in their work. If you want to honor them, buy some of the stuff they made. That way you get to experience them at their best and you also give their heirs a few extra bucks to keep the family name alive. And for God's sake, if you feel compelled to visit the graves of Jim Morrison or John Belushi or some other dead addict, don't leave the detritus of the substances that killed them to "honor their memory"—it's in poor taste. If you must follow their paths that religiously, use that shit yourself, then listen to their music or watch their movies or whatever. You'll finally *hear* Jimi and no one will have to worry about stepping on your broken Jack Daniels bottles or razor blades while traipsing through a graveyard to visit their dipshit Everest-climbing dad's mausoleum.

FUCK IT:
I'M NOT GOING TO WATCH ANDY WARHOL'S *EMPIRE*

From what I gather from my hoity-toity friends, *Empire* is an eight-hour-long continuous slow-motion shot of the Empire State Building, filmed during the night of July 25, into July 26, in 1964. The sun goes down, the floodlights on the building come up and eventually, after about six and a half hours, the screen is pretty much—to co-opt the late George Carlin's weather forecast for tonight—dark.

My verdict on this? If I wanted to spend eight hours staring at a screen full of predictable nothingness I'd watch Fox News.

FUCK IT:
I'M NOT GOING TO WALK THE CAMINO

I'd been watching a yoga class through a window at my gym—attracted by an angelic lady instructor but sustained by a lithe, limber, salt-and-pepper-haired man who stood on his head and pointed his toes at the ceiling like a fleshy bullet. He was so impressively peaceful. As people exited the class, I feigned post-workout stretches, so as not to appear the creep that I was, and heard Bulletfoot tell someone he had recently "walked the Camino." Thinking I had heard, "I bought a Camaro," I fleshy-bulleted over to the group of now five or six surrounding the man who went on to describe a long walk he had taken. "Why would you walk if you have a Camaro?" I asked. Everyone looked at me with disdain. Except for the man, who offered me a beatific (read: condescending) smile and said in an accent that belied his pasty demeanor, "Cah-ME-no." Turns out "walking the Cah-ME-no" is common parlance for a pilgrimage to the shrine of a dead saint (is there any other kind?) in Spain. "Vroom vroom!" I said, making a motorcycle-throttling gesture with my hands, blowing a raspberry and motoring my imaginary hog on out of there.

FUCK IT:
I'M NOT GETTING MARRIED

When it's working well, marriage is a kick-ass institution. There are, of course, so many positives associated with the word "institution." For example, "an organization, establishment, foundation, society or the like, devoted to the promotion of a particular cause or program, especially one of a public, educational or charitable character." Marriage is commitment. And marriage is an institution. You are *committed to an institution*. 'Til death do you part.

FUCK IT:
I'M NOT GOING TO VISIT ALL FIFTY STATES

I've been to a whole lot of states in this country already. I've driven I-70 all night and into the dawn more than once. I've found myself in Texas or Washington and even a retirement community in Florida. I've got a lot of America underneath my big leather belt. Aside from Alaska and Hawaii though, I'm pretty much done with it. I've seen enough. Or, put another way, I simply don't believe America has much else to show me. I'd love to be proven wrong. But I don't think I will be. So, okay, I'll try a few more states—eat your local BBQ or whatever else I could have just as easily run over with my car, wrapped in tinfoil and cooked up on my engine manifold. Some states have so little uniqueness to offer that they come up with things like the "World's Largest Ball of String" or a truck stop with a fifty-foot statue of Paul Bunyan, just to get you to detour off I-80 and spend some greenbacks on a life-sized jackalope dressed up in Duck Dynasty camouflage. They're home to roadside attractions where you can hang out wondering what you're doing there while posing for photos with all the other people who went one hundred miles out of their way to witness "America's Tallest Outhouse."

"Don't leave! You haven't seen America's Largest Roll of Toilet Paper yet!"

FUCK IT:
I'M NOT GOING TO MEET MY SOULMATE

Soulmates are an illusion. This is your mind playing tricks on you. It lasts for a while, then you are left with reality. Most love is a chemical in your brain. It wears out. Then you are left with someone who thinks it's funny to cropdust a fart in Wal-Mart and walk away. Most people who think they've found their soulmate do it when they have lots of free time and no interruptions. Then real life takes over. About 50 percent of marriages end in divorce. How many of those people think a judge handed their house to their soulmate?

FUCK IT:
I'M NOT TAKING A COOKING CLASS

You know one of the benefits of having a decent job? Being able to go out to a nice dinner every once in a while. If I took a cooking class and, God forbid, excelled at it, I could risk losing one pleasure that's already been confirmed: eating better food at restaurants than I have at home. I'm sorry, Jiro's dreams of sushi collapse under the weight of the juicy filet mignon waiting for me at Tournedos Steakhouse this evening.

FUCK IT:
I'M NOT GOING TO THE PLAYBOY MANSION

The Playboy Mansion is a symbol, a logo, a complex message packed into a single estate. It promises debauchery, raw sex, uninhibited partying, no consequences and that what happens at the mansion—as they say—stays at the mansion. But the truth is that the Playboy Mansion doesn't exist at all. It is a building made of bricks and mortar, yes, but the true Playboy Mansion is a Platonic ideal generated by the unbridled adolescent male id. That, and I'd most certainly be the third wheel in the Nicky Minaj-à-trois and get kicked off the plush, heart-shaped bed. The Playboy Mansion is a fantasy whose time has come and gone. It hasn't been cool since eight-track players. Not to mention the hot tub at the Playboy Mansion is nicknamed "The Hollywood Sperm Bank."

FUCK IT:
I'M NOT GOING TO CATCH A GREASED PIG

I eat bacon and ham sandwiches and probably other pig byproducts I don't even realize I'm eating. I don't want to be a hypocrite. But coating a pig in oil and chasing it around some county fairground while deep-fried carnival-food-bloated spectators cheer from the sidelines seems particularly cruel and unusual—even for a carnivore. A team of researchers from Newcastle University's School of Agriculture, Food and Rural Development conducted tests on pigs and concluded that they can feel "optimistic and pessimistic according to how they are treated." Thus, in the case of greased-pig catching, I'm going to conclude that the pigs will feel pessimistic about the whole enterprise, not to mention terrified. Other studies have concluded that pigs have the same mental capacity as a three-year-old human. I'm guessing that most of the members of 4-H clubs or the attendees of county fairs where greased-pig chases are typically held would not cotton to having their kids greased up and chased by adults for entertainment, no matter how delicious the little fuckers may be.

FUCK IT:
I'M NOT GOING TO WALK THE EDGE OF THE CN TOWER

How is this even legal? The goddamn tower is nearly two thousand feet tall, smack in the middle of downtown Toronto. The fact that people want to be tethered to an overhead rail system and walk around the outside edge of it absolutely blows my mind. It's the tallest free-standing structure in the Western Hemisphere and these people pay to walk on the *outside* of it. I went up in the CN Tower once. They have a glass observation window built into the floor and when I looked down through it I almost passed out—and I wasn't at the edge of anything!

Even more shocking: They let kids as young as thirteen walk out on the edge. In fact, they've got a hip, youthful name that goes along with the activity—they call it "EdgeWalk"—that seems custom-built to attract teenagers. IMO, that name is the Joe Camel of thrill-seeking. Sure, the kids have to be accompanied by an adult, but whatever. Any parent or guardian who would let their thirteen-year-old walk around the edge of the CN Tower is an abomination. Don't even get me started on people who get married up there. If you need that much excitement at the beginning of your marriage, you've got a long, painful road ahead of you.

FUCK IT:
I'M NOT GOING TO COSTA RICA
TO WATCH TURTLES HATCH ON THE BEACH

It's called the Discovery Channel, folks. I saw turtle eggs hatch and a couple lions going to town on a crocodile and wrote a book all in the very same day.

FUCK IT:
I'M NOT LEARNING HOW TO SHOOT POOL

I've heard it said that knowing how to shoot pool is the sure sign of a misspent youth. Personally, I burned through my youth like a napalm-dipped Roman candle, but I still can't make a bank shot. That's cool—I'm content to plant myself on a stool three feet from a side pocket and watch a pro go to work. I may never master the game myself, but the beer will be cold enough, sleep will come easily, and the clack of balls will be a rhythmic Celtic poem to my drunken Irish ears.

FUCK IT:
I'M NOT GOING TO BECOME AN ORDAINED MINISTER

As an ordained minister, you can officiate wedding ceremonies, funerals, and other important ceremonies. You can hop on the Internet and become an ordained Universal Life Minister for free. It might be worth it, even if it's just to hear confessions. "That's a lot of sins, young lady. Meet me at the Holiday Inn and I'll tell you your penance."

It would be fun to be able to marry people. It's just that I don't trust myself—I can't be sure that I won't do a little improv while I'm at it. "If anyone feels this couple should not be united in holy matrimony, speak now or forever hold your peace." I'd be awfully tempted to wait a few beats and say, astonished, "Really? No one? No ex-boyfriends? No ex-girlfriends? Nobody? Last chance! Okay then. You may now French kiss the bride and cop a feel."

FUCK IT:
I'M NOT TAKING THE NEXT FLIGHT WHEREVER IT'S GOING

Seriously. People do this. What are the odds that some random flight will be going anywhere that I'd remotely like to spend time? My ball-breathable Bermuda shorts and flip-flops would be of no use to me in fuckin' Vladivostok.

FUCK IT:
I'M NOT LEARNING HOW TO SNOWBOARD

Because I remember when two skis were the only option. Because skiing is one thing and surfing is another and never the two shall meet. Because given the option between "go big" and "go home," I choose the latter. Because I don't want a hat that looks like a dragon's tail, and I don't want flame designs on anything that I wear, and I don't have the patience to learn a whole new language to describe jumps and flips I'll never be able to do anyway. Because winter is for hibernation. Because it's called après-ski not après-board. Because I'm neither a "dude" nor a "bro," nor do I wish to "bro down" with anyone under any circumstance. Because wrists break oh-so-easily. Because my center of gravity is as high as my motivation is low. Not to mention, a halfpipe sounds like something for smoking half your weed.

FUCK IT:
I'M NOT GOING TO BURNING MAN

I've heard the stories from friends who become more and more dis-
enchanted every single year. I actually look forward to their evolv-
ing annual recap. Reminds me of how justified I felt when, after
one misspent New Year's, I resisted the bullying of "friends" who
urged me to repeat the mistake of spending $150 for an evening of
unlimited chicken wings and Nattie Light. These invites went on
for years. "The whole festival has really changed and lost its soul,
man," is the usual Burner review. "You feel me? It used to be about
art and freedom and experimentation and bailing out on money-
worshipping bourgeois culture. But now it's all segregated into the
haves and have nots just like the rest of the filthy, wretched western
world. You feel me?" I feel you, I feel you. I miss Jerry Garcia too,
my brother. But I'm still not going to Burning Man.

Every functioning alcoholic I talked to about their Fuck It list had a variation on this theme:

> Drink Scotch in Scotland
> Drink Guinness in Ireland
> Drink Vodka in Russia
> Drink Burgundy in France
> Drink Absinthe in Paris
> Drink Mead in Egypt

Chances are if you're such a lush that these are on your bucket list, you've either got a trust fund or you're broke and can't afford the trip. You may want to back off before your bucket list includes "Drink mouthwash at CVS."

FUCK IT:
I'M NOT LEARNING HOW TO POLE DANCE

Let me tell you something pretty much every heterosexual American male learns firsthand by the age of twenty-three (and twenty-three is what I'd call a late bloomer): Pole dancing is for strippers. Spin it around whatever pole you want. At my advanced age of something-something, I remember the thinly veiled eroticism of the early Jane Fonda aerobics videos: the mule kicks and arching back that created all sorts of intriguing dromedary hoof activity across the front of her leotard. Remember, this was back before the Internet, when teenage boys would have to watch the scrambled HBO and Showtime signals for a fleeting hint of nipple. Ms. Fonda was innovating exercise for women who just wanted to be in positions that women want to be in. Pole dancing was something *completely* different. Think about it—why do people take pole dancing classes? Exercise is a long shot. To feel sexy? I'll buy that—if sexy is performing in a sticky-seated cabaret starring women with horrible fathers who are trying to "put themselves through med school." And, in case anyone is wondering, men who take pole dancing classes to be sexy are not interested in the women there.

FUCK IT:
I'LL NEVER RIDE A BULLET TRAIN

Trains roll past my tall apartment windows every thirty minutes. They're no more than twenty yards away and often stop directly outside my windows to back up, wait, switch tracks—do loud train things—then squeak and grind to life with unimaginable effort. You might think that having loud trains pass so close by at such regular intervals would be an annoyance, but it's not. These are old trains, working trains, transport trains hauling God knows what to who knows where, and the men hanging off them are railroad men. They climb in and out of locomotive cabs, and lean down to inspect immense steel wheels and cogs, and they shine flashlights and wave those lights and wave their hands, signaling so the trains can groan back to work. The cars are covered with graffiti, each a rolling art gallery of street style, brash primary colors, braggadocio. Each signature design taps into an urge—an all-consuming artistic urge—to create moveable art for people the artist will never see in places they'll never visit. I am spoiled by this rolling art gallery. I am spoiled by bearing witness to the train schedules, their work; I'm a silent observer of the steady metal behemoths that crawl past my window, marking time better than the sun, reminding me how some of us grind forward making what we need to make, getting where we need to go, chugging down the tracks no matter what, even if we have to stop, roll backwards, and readjust before moving forward.

FUCK IT:
I'M NOT RIDING A MOTORCYCLE CROSS COUNTRY

Frankly, I love this one as a concept. Out on the open highway, punching through an 80 mph wind on a bike built sleek and solid for cruising long hauls. But here's the thing: A helmet, leather jacket and motorcycle boots can't replace the protection of a big steel cage with airbags and shatterproof glass. So instead of a motorcycle, I'd prefer to drive a Volvo wagon cross country. Riding cross country on a motorcycle sounds exciting and even kinda romantic in a Marlon Brando sorta way when you're telling other people about it. Personally though, I'm happy that car-seat technology has come a long way. Lumbar support. Heated seats. Headrests. I would think that after about two hundred miles, the haunting prospect of sitting on a cow-milking stool for another 2,800 miles loses its luster.

FUCK IT:
I'M NOT GOING TO RUN A MARATHON

"26.2" bumper stickers are more annoying than those "Baby on Board" ones from the eighties. I can't be the only one who wants to T-bone any car emblazoned with one. If you want to run a marathon before you croak, fine, go for it, but keep it to yourself. What if everyone who fulfilled their dream of having a three-way drove around with a "Middle ménager at 3way.com" sticker on their car? "I ♥ Riding Crop Floggings!"; "ORGY ACCOMPLISHED"; "Bi-Curious + Bi-Experienced = Bi-Satisfied"—quit bragging.

FUCK IT:
I'M NOT GOING TO COMIC-CON

Did you know that Comic-Con International is a "nonprofit educational corporation dedicated to creating awareness of, and appreciation for, comics and related popular artforms"? Me neither. See, that's the problem with stuff like Comic-Con. You take a perfectly good gathering of like-minded obsessives and try to justify it by elevating it into something meaningful like an educational entity. Tell me how, exactly, viewing exclusive trailers of the latest Hollywood blockbuster alien film qualifies as educational rather than promotional? Or how dressing up as an obscure minor character from a video game you've spent hundreds of hours playing alone in your basement enlightens anyone at all? Does getting a signed photograph of George Takei really move our species forward a step? It would be nice if it did. Then I could feel more justified about the signed Captain Hikaru Sulu poster I'm staring at as I type this in my basement. Besides, I probably wouldn't get in. I'm not a virgin.

FUCK IT:
I'M NOT RIDING A MULE TO THE
BOTTOM OF THE GRAND CANYON

I asked a friend who'd done this once whether he would recommend it to anyone. His response was chilling. Apparently, he was assigned a mule that had runny eyes and more flies around it than an outhouse in August. The animal was sick, dirty, and too old to be doing such work. As such, it wasn't too interested in walking. When my friend complained to the mule wrangler, he was handed a two-foot-long leather whip known in the industry, apparently, as a "motivator." He was told to "motivate" the mule up and down the canyon until the trip was complete. When he balked, the wrangler laughed and mocked him for his hesitation. "That's adorable," he said. My friend, the poor bastard, caved and beat the damn mule all day and most of the next, his justifying mantra, "this hurts me more than it hurts you." The trip has haunted this guy ever since. He can be found on most evenings whispering apologies into the ear of the mechanical bull at Whiskey River.

FUCK IT:
I'M NOT GOING ON A SINGLES CRUISE

I was in the sweet spot for watching *The Love Boat*. The series started in the late 1970s, prime-time on Saturday night, and I was just old enough to feel titillated by its sexual innuendos, but too young to judge its formidable hokeyness. To this day, when I hear about someone taking a cruise, I picture Captain Merrill Stubing in his starched white uniform and Julie "Your Cruise Director" in her official blue blazer, welcoming them onto the ship. There is an abundance of sexual adventure in the air. At some point, Charo will shake her hips suggestively, the ship's doctor will proposition every woman on board, and fruity cocktails will be served by a grinning young man sporting a robust mustache. Whether or not the passengers got lucky on that show, the crew seemed to be up to their epaulets in hanky-panky. I say if you want to go on a cruise to get laid, more power to you. Set a course for adventure, your mind on a new romance. Just keep in mind the average denizen of these cruises has exhausted every place on dry land and every dating site on the Internet looking for a mate. My own experience could never be sexier than the cruise-ship fantasies I've been harboring since those Saturday nights of my childhood.

FUCK IT:
I'M NOT WALKING THE GREAT WALL OF CHINA

In 1988, the performance artist Marina Abramović and her on-again-off-again boyfriend, artist Uwe Laysiepen, ended their relationship with a grand romantic gesture. Laysiepen started from the Gobi Desert, Abramović started from the Yellow Sea, and together, yet on their own, they walked 1,500 miles to break up in the middle of the Great Wall of China. They did this because, as Abramović said, "in the end you are really alone, whatever you do." The magic of the Great Wall, which has been fortified countless times over the centuries with everything from stone to brick to wood to tamped earth, and thus a symbol of strength, solidarity, and union, wasn't enough to fend off a couple of commitment-phobic attention seekers from huffing and puffing and, I imagine, power texting "i wanna brk up, MEt me @d gr8 Wall" that wall down.

FUCK IT:
I'M NOT GETTING INTO
THE GUINNESS BOOK OF WORLD RECORDS

Meh. Why bother?

FUCK IT:
I'M NOT GOING TO MUNICH FOR OKTOBERFEST

There's only so much lederhosen and accordion music a person can take. And thanks to cargo ships, we can get German beer here, and there are Oktoberfests all over the USA. Perhaps I'm diminishing the cultural importance, but ever since I passed my heavy drinking days this event doesn't seem that appealing. In fact, it seems sweaty and crowded and bloated and vaguely like Wisconsin.

FUCK IT:
I'M NOT LEARNING HOW TO PLAY PIANO

It's not so much learning to tinkle on the keys, which actually does seem like fun—it's that the whole enterprise of taking piano lessons usually involves a recital in some dry YMCA auditorium, where you, along with an itinerary of other piano students, waterboard torture family and friends with simple tunes you make your way through like an apologetic hand job.

Every time I see a Facebook video of a four-year-old playing Rachmaninoff's Symphony no. 2 I am reminded that piano is something you have to start playing young. Oh, and while I'm at it—Keith Urban's guitar-lesson infomercial isn't very appealing either.

FUCK IT:
I'M NOT GOING TO KNIT A SCARF

Picture a sweet old biddy working on some sort of ducky pattern with fuzzy yellow yarn. She's wearing bifocals and chunky black support shoes, and she's rocking back and forth in a creaky rocking chair, humming the lullaby from *Jocelyn* and smiling about the twelve grandchildren around the country for whom she's knitting sweaters, booties, and winter hats. The scene is beautiful. Unless the biddy is a 6'3" man in his mid-forties with a goatee and a dagger tattoo on his forearm.

FUCK IT:
I'M NOT RIDING THE SIX BIGGEST ROLLER COASTERS

This seems like a bucket list holdover from adolescence, because this is an activity that should be on your bucket list when you're fourteen—and ticked off by the time you're thirty. No one should be on a roller coaster after fifty. Just look at the scary warning signs at the entrance. Cautionary advisories include, "Do not ride if you have a heart condition." Gee, what a great way to find out if you have a heart condition. "Do not ride if you are prone to motion sickness or dizziness." Really? There's going to be motion on this ride? Thanks for the heads-up.

I'm especially fond of "Do not ride if you are pregnant." That one must be for the same people who need to be advised in TV commercials that "Viagra does not stop the spread of HIV or other sexually transmitted diseases." Then there's the most politically correctly worded warning: "Due to the restrictive nature of this ride's restraints, guests with unique body proportions may not be able to safely ride." In other words, "Go win a teddy bear at the ring toss, Lardo."

"No thanks" on the roller coasters. I'm scared enough being upside down on my mortgage. I'd have a lot more fun staying home watching Mike Rowe on *Dirty Jobs*, trying to mop corn-dog and kettle-corn vomit off the Satan's Bullet ride.

FUCK IT:
I'M NOT DRIVING A FORMULA ONE CAR

It's entertaining watching cars race as fast as they can around in circles—dogs and laser pointers, I get it. It would be fun driving around sexy Monaco at warp speeds. It would be even more fun meeting all the European women who get turned on by death-defying Formula One drivers. I'd love to play baccarat at a Monaco casino with four supermodels cheering me on. But here's something most people don't realize: Formula One cockpits are *really* small. Most of these guys could be jockeys. I get claustrophobic on a bus. And that's without hearing the words "wall," "two hundred miles an hour," and "burst into flames" all in one sentence.

FUCK IT:
I'M NOT GOING TO THE SUPER BOWL

I'm one of those guys who never learned about football and now it's too late. There's an entire male world, entire nights' worth of conversation, that I'm excluded from—and, for the most part, I've come to terms with that. I simply avoid sports conversations whenever possible.

But I'm always amused by the rabid football fans. Do they realize that if they'd been born and raised in a different city they'd be rabid fans of *that* team instead? After the big win the spectators flood the streets, drunken men wearing other men's names on their shirts, not unlike high-school girls wearing their boyfriend's varsity jackets when they're going steady. They climb lampposts and basically riot in the streets, screaming, "We won! We won!" You did *not* win. The guys on the field won. You paid $500 to sit in the nosebleed section of the stadium eating hot dogs and praying all the while that the wind would pick up enough for you to sneak out a beer fart without getting caught.

FUCK IT:
I'M NOT GOING TO START A CHARITY

The problem here is deciding which issue to get behind. There are so many choices, each more horrible than the next. Poverty, environmental destruction, disease, famine, domestic violence . . . the world is a veritable smorgasbord of bad shit that needs fixing. But really, aren't Bill Gates and Bono doing enough for all of us?

FUCK IT:
I'M NOT GOING TO SAIL THROUGH
THE BERMUDA TRIANGLE

No fucking way. I believe all that shit. Bermuda Triangle . . . alien probes . . . mermaid skeletons washed up on the beach . . . Bigfoot . . . the Loch Ness Monster . . . all of it. Give me any sort of story about inexplicable occurrences or show me a grainy photograph of some possibly physical shape emerging from a cloud bank and I'll believe any theory you want to throw at it. I'm not saying this because I'm proud of it. I'm saying it because I know this about myself. Whacknut myths and conspiracy theories are my intellectual Achilles' Heel. So when you tell me you want to sail through the Bermuda Triangle don't be surprised when I tell you you're fucking crazy, Amelia Earhart.

FUCK IT:
I'M NOT GOING TO DO STAND-UP COMEDY

There are several reasons why you should not do stand-up comedy, no matter how often your friends say, "You're really funny—you should do stand-up!" First off: They're lying. Second off: They're wrong. You are going to suck at it for years and years. You are not as funny as you think you are. And neither am I. No one is as funny as they think they are. That's why there are so many divorces. Fat jokes don't go over well in bed. "I love your waterbed! Oh, that's you? Sorry."

Also, the law of supply and demand is not in your favor. There are a gazillion open mics everywhere, filled with wannabe comedians disappointing their parents. The dismissively sarcastic statement "everybody's a comedian" has never been so true as it is now. There are no audiences left because everyone on Facebook and Twitter is a performer. "Look at me! Look at what I ate! Look at my cat—he's soooo cute! Aren't I funny?" No, you are not. Your friends don't really care if you're funny. They care if you think *they're* funny. Click "Like" if you agree.

Perhaps you want to try it as a way to challenge your fears. A way to face your fear of public speaking. And that's good. Life is better when you push your personal boundaries. Stripping naked in a bowling alley will challenge your fears just as well, but it'll also get you on a sex offender registry. Still, please, for the love of God and all that is holy don't become a comedian.

Being clever is highly overrated. I suggest you try needlepoint. People who do needlepoint aren't desperate for approval. Relax. Live your life with an appreciation for the people who have reached the highest level of their profession. As the stock heckler response goes, "Don't give me a hard time. I don't come down to where you work and kick the mop out of your hand, do I?"

FUCK IT:
I'M NOT GOING TO DUBLIN FOR BLOOMSDAY

James Joyce set his novel on June 16, 1904, to commemorate his first date with his future wife, Nora Barnacle (thanks for the surname, Mom and Pop Bill Barnacle), and thus this is the date when *Ulysses* obsessives take to the streets to celebrate a date that ended in a hand job. "The greatest novel of the last century is also a monument to perhaps the lowliest of sex acts—one not even deserving of its own Latinate nickname, like *coitus* or *fellatio*," writes James Murphy in *Vanity Fair*. "A hand job is vulgar, sloppy, and juvenile, much like the book it inspired is at its best." Yeah, that about covers it.

FUCK IT:
I'M NOT FLYING TO PARIS FOR DINNER

I've never been this hungry nor this romantic.

FUCK IT:
I'M NOT GOING TO SPRING BREAK IN DAYTONA

As Austin Powers once said, "Unfortunately, for yours truly, that train has sailed." At my age—hell, at your age—we're either gonna look like narcs or pervs down there, depending on our haircuts. And where your haircut is located. And, for that matter, whether it's shaped like a heart or a four-leaf clover. George Bernard Shaw famously said, "Youth is wasted on the young." I believe in observing Spring Break in Daytona we might best shorten that to, "Youth is wasted." I don't want to be a part of any rite of passage that includes falling from a hotel balcony. I didn't like drunken frat boys when I was in college, and I don't expect I will find that has changed. When Daniel fled the lions' den, he didn't go back for his hat.

FUCK IT:
I'M NOT GOING TO BUNGEE JUMP

I suppose this is exciting to some people—Jumping like a human yo-yo off a bridge with large stationery supplies (i.e., rubber bands) strapped to your ankles. I imagine it's quite an adrenaline rush. You may want to try it. You may even want to do it in Australia over the Zambezi River at Victoria Falls, the world's largest water-fall. Now *that* would be awesome. I suggest you Google "Erin Langworthy 360-foot plunge crocodile-infested river" before you make your reservations.

FUCK IT:
I'M NOT GOING TO GROW DREADLOCKS

I came very close at one time. I was following the Grateful Dead around the country in a VW camper and my hair went from 'fro to tangled mop to clumping on the brink of dreadlocks. In truth, there was a nice little patch of dreads at the base of my neck—I even cut off the biggest one and saved it for posterity, but for the life of me I can't remember where I stashed it. In other words, somewhere among my piles of old concert tickets and tattered Guatemalan shirts there is a turd-like biscuit of hair that disproves the entire premise of this particular Fuck It. Dreadlocks look pretty good on some Jamaican Rastas. But if *you* grow them, you may just want to buy a T-shirt with big block letters that read: "I HAVE WEED."

FUCK IT:
I'M NOT TRYING VEGETARIANISM

If there were any experience that would turn me vegetarian it would've been the temp job working in a meat-packing plant. As an untrained, temporary laborer, my main task was to lug tubes of meat from one processing station to another. It was my first experience with meat outside of a grocery store, and seeing the substance in a form more suitable for a building supply than a lunch menu was almost enough to turn me off of meat for good. Almost.

I don't have a problem with vegetarians until they start talking like Jehovah's Witnesses trying to convert me. To each his own— but I like meat. Big, fat, juicy steaks. If cows didn't want us to eat them, they should have evolved with opposable thumbs to fend us off with rocks.

FUCK IT:
I'M NOT GOING TO LEARN TO PLAY POKER

On the night I played my first hand of poker, I was told an old piece of gambler's wisdom that has stuck with me ever since: If you don't know who the sucker at the table is, it's you. I folded my cards, walked away from the table, and haven't been back since.

Also, it takes years to become a good card player. If you have any desire to become a professional poker player, just go to a casino on Christmas and see all the lonely people. You'll fold that fantasy on the spot.

I have a little pet theory that married men like to play poker because it provides them with the feeling of being right sometimes. That's the real reward. Every time you win a hand, the victory cancels out times like when you wanted to see the new James Bond flick and your wife wanted to see *The Notebook*. Incidentally, Ryan Gosling was terrific.

FUCK IT:
I'M NOT LEARNING HOW TO SKATEBOARD

My grandparents were snowbirds cruising in a slipstream between Rochester, NY, and Fort Lauderdale, FL. It was the mid-seventies and I was the baby of the family and skateboards hadn't hit upstate New York yet. My grandparents brought back two of them—plastic gray decks and primitive ball-bearing wheels—all so narrow that even my little feet could barely stand side by side. They were so foreign and un-upstate-like, those sleek gray Makos my brothers tried to master while rumbling over the cracked black-topped suburban driveway, as if California and New York could flip places with one perfectly placed push-kick and elegantly carved turn. They rode with no knee pads, no elbow pads, and no helmets. Danger is like catnip to boys. I'm not learning now—as if skateboarding could ever get better than it was in the 1970s!

FUCK IT:
I'M NOT GOING TO RUN FOR PUBLIC OFFICE

Unless you are a millionaire or your family has sent their kids to Harvard or Yale for five generations, you will never get near Congress or the Senate. If your bucket list includes holding public office, you'll be lucky to get on the school board in your town. Or get elected to your town council. There's something quite sad about conning your friends into putting up a sign with your name on it in their front yard. This isn't "your name up in lights," this is your name on cheap cardboard next to a rusty bicycle some kid left in the rain for a year. Your dreams of being a mover and a shaker, a political powerbroker, someone very important, will be relegated to organizing bake sales, designing T-shirts for 5K runs and begging your neighbors to vote for you. Which isn't to say serving on a school board isn't honorable. Service to children is an honorable calling. Just don't expect it to be anything like the dream most politicians have of people kissing their asses and sending them on junkets to the Caribbean so they'll give the good people funding for a new football stadium.

FUCK IT:
I'M NOT GROWING UP

We grow so old and strange. To each other. To ourselves. To our children. To our grandchildren. A walking museum of grotesqueries—the accumulated weight of habits, compulsions, bad decisions and the like distorting our features, lengthening our ears, twisting our pointer fingers back at ourselves when they were once so comfortable pointing at others. And me, I have Peter Pan Syndrome. I admit it. I will resist growing old at all costs—with the exception of lipo, face lifts, hair transplants, or a toupee. Especially a bad toupee. A bad toupee, of course, looks bad. But the real flaw in wearing a bad toupee is that it tells people that your mind and your sense of reality are so shot that you believe you're getting away with it. I'm talking to you, Donald Trump.

FUCK IT:
I'M NOT GOING TO RIDE IN A HOT AIR BALLOON

Such whimsy, isn't it, the juxtaposition of flame and fabric, basket and rope, floating and flying through the bluest sky without a care in the world. During a bleary-eyed Daniel Craig movie marathon I saw the 2004 flick *Enduring Love*. The inciting incident was a hot air balloon accident. No, I would not like to ride up, up, and away in your beautiful balloon.

FUCK IT:
I'M NOT GOING TO QUIT WORK

I had the incredibly good fortune to be born a solidly middle class white male in America. I was also born in Generation X, a generation known for carving out its own niches and saying things like, "Do what you love. Love what you do." While I sometimes whine just like everyone else, it would be the height of arrogance to truly complain about my work. I do, indeed, do what I love and love what I do, which, at the moment, is ridiculing your bucket lists.

FUCK IT:
I'M NOT GOING TO WRITE A BOOK

Save yourself, my friends.
It's too late for me.